A Place to Talk *in*
Pack-away Settings

'It's true, sometimes we just can't see the wood for the trees. Not only does Elizabeth Jarman provide the inspiration and incentive for early years education and childcare practititioners to stop, look and take stock, she demonstrates how both the wood and the trees can be used to create magical thinking spaces that can't fail to be irresistible to children and adults alike!'

Kay Errington, Early Years Service Manager
Bournemouth Borough Council

A Place to Talk *in* Pack-away Settings

Elizabeth Jarman

Reprinted 2009 (twice)
Published 2009 by A&C Black Publishers Limited
36 Soho Square, London W1D 3QY
www.acblack.com

First published 2008 by Featherstone Education Limited

ISBN 978-1-9060-2926-5

Text © Elizabeth Jarman
Photographs © Elizabeth Jarman

A CIP record for this publication is available from the British Library.

Printed in Great Britain by Martins the Printers, Berwick-upon-Tweed

This book is produced using paper that is made from wood grown in
managed, sustainable forests. It is natural, renewable and recyclable.
The logging and manufacturing processes conform to the environmental
regulations of the country of origin.

To see our full range of titles
visit www.acblack.com

Introduction

The recent I CAN report[1] suggests that over 50% of children in England are starting school with some form of speech and language difficulty or disability. The Early Years Foundation Stage reinforces that "the development and use of communication and language is at the heart of young children's learning."[2] Improving children's speaking and listening skills, has never been so important.

This resource considers the significant role that the physical environment can play in supporting children's speaking and listening skills; in supporting inquisitive, verbal experimentation, not just answering questions!

It includes a summary of some of the key environmental influences, collated from research studies; it includes lots of examples of what this looks like in practice; it poses questions to prompt action and it sign-posts you to further information.

We hope that this resource will challenge and inspire practitioners working in Pack-away Settings to create really effective 'places to talk'.

Developed alongside key Early Years developments, for example Every Child Matters, the Early Years Foundation Stage and Communicating Matters, 'A Place to Talk' has been recognised as an exciting and informative tool.

[1] *Cost to the Nation,* I CAN, 2006

[2] QCA/DfES: Curriculum Guidance for the Foundation Stage, p45

Contents

A Place to Talk *in* Pack-away Settings

Five environmental factors to consider

Following a review of research and practice in Early Years settings across England and Wales, we have identified five really important environmental points to consider when creating spaces designed to encourage children's speaking and listening skills.

> 1. *The physical environment should reflect the pedagogy[3] of the setting.*

Establishing a shared team understanding of your pedagogy will inform the way that you plan your learning environment. The way that a physical space is arranged says a lot to children about what is expected there and the sort of interactions welcome. It's really important that the learning environment and pedagogy connect and support one another.

> 2. *Practitioners should make the most of the space available, both inside and out.*

It's important to view learning spaces as a whole, including both inside and out and make the most of what's available. Across the space, children need secure spaces to talk where they feel comfortable and relaxed.

> 3. *Spaces should take account of physical factors that can impact on learning; for example, noise, colour and light.*

Noise

Being in a noisy environment makes it really difficult for children to concentrate. This can have a negative effect on their speaking and listening skills.

Colour

Colours need to be chosen carefully as they can affect children's behaviour and ability to focus and engage in conversation.

---

[3] *pedagogy* is your 'teaching' style

Light

Current research confirms that we are all energized by natural sunlight and that children learn faster in spaces with natural light. Light can be used to create mood and define an area.

4. The environment should not be over stimulating.

Too much choice can be overwhelming. Storage options should therefore be carefully considered.

The purpose and positioning of displays needs review. For example, it makes sense not to have a busy, cluttered display in an area where children are expected to focus say on a story book at group time.

5. Spaces should be viewed from the child's perspective.

Informed by a thorough understanding of how language develops we should keenly observe what the children are actually doing and how they are responding to the spaces we create, in order to plan appropriate, flexible environments that stimulate speaking and listening skills.

Twelve ideas to try

Inspired by practice from many settings, we have created twelve 'places to talk' that reflect the five environmental factors.

Each idea is spread over two pages:

➤ There is a 'starter' photograph of the space and a description of how we created it.

➤ We have included key points about why we chose those particular materials, why we positioned the furniture as we did and so on.

➤ There are also some photographs of children using the space, with their comments and some observations of what they did.

➤ We have included some action points for you to consider.

You'll see that what we are talking about does not have to cost a fortune, in fact you may already have some of the materials and resources that we have used. What it does involve though, is an informed view, keen observation skills which inform planning, so that you create the sort of environment that reflects what you want for children in your setting.

We acknowledge that opportunities for speaking and listening are everywhere, and we hope that these ideas will inspire you to review and develop some special 'places to talk' in your setting.

An quiet space to explore

How and why?

We set this space up to offer a quiet place for children to withdraw to. We wanted to offer a place where they could observe other activity in the outside area. We attached a voile hanging from the branches of a tree in a quiet part of the garden, which created an instant enclosed space. We added a circular rug so that it was more comfortable and a basket containing interesting textured materials. We deliberately kept it simple as 'over resourcing' spaces can make them feel cluttered and overwhelming.

Olivia explored the collection of materials, which had sensory appeal. She smelled the wood, held the paper thin leaves up to the light to look at their patterns. She rubbed the bark, "It's all crunchy like carrots," she said. She was using all of her senses and used complex comparative language.

She enjoyed being in the enclosed space, sitting and watching the others.

Action

Do you have any quiet spaces where children can 'watch' from? Are they comfortable and inviting? What sort of interesting collections could you add to add sensory appeal?

Well presented resources, worth investigating

How and why?

We set up a collection of gourds on a small, low table in a quiet area. We presented them in a simple 'grid like container' for the children to find.

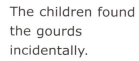

The children found the gourds incidentally.

"Where you get this stuff?" asked Luke.

"It grew in the ground, Luke," I said.

He looked at me and the gourds very suspiciously, having never seen anything like them before and asked slowly, "Which ground?"

Lots of touching, weighing, holding and thinking were triggered along with descriptive language and lots of talk. The presentation of the resources worked well as the children could clearly see the gourds. They were a really engaging resource and worth spending time exploring.

Action

What sort of resources do you have that children would find as interesting? Natural objects can offer so much more appeal and fascination than plastic. Next time you are replacing resources think about adding some collections of natural materials and how you could present them to draw children in.

A space for stories

How and why?

We set up this story space using child height folding chairs, a wigwam, made from garden canes, a sheet and a folding unit to display the books. The circular mats leading into the area help to define the space. The cats add a point of interest.

So often, book areas are cluttered with too many books on offer. If books are not presented well, in a manageable way then children can learn to disrespect them and in fact it makes it really hard for the child who wants to find their favourite story for you to re read again and again.

This space is uncluttered and calm. The books are well presented. There are different spaces where children can read; in an enclosed space, on the chairs or on the mats. The area isn't plastered in bright posters and information, which can often make story areas over stimulating and make it difficult for children to focus.

Action

Look at your story area. Does it feel calm and inviting? Would you like to spend time relaxing with a book in there? Do you need to thin out the books and present them more effectively?

An enclosed space

How and why?

We set up a tent and folding camping chair, with a sleeping bag, cushions and some blankets in a quieter area of the garden. We positioned the entrance to make the space look inviting, but used the chair to add privacy, positioning it so that it backed onto the rest of the garden. The colours of the space blended in to the natural setting, creating a calm area where children could play.

Olivia and Reece were wary of the space at first and needed 'permission' to go inside. The modelling and support from the staff member helped with this and they then took the play forward independently. The interaction from outside to inside the tent was interesting to watch and the position of being on the chair somehow gave Olivia authority to direct what would happen next.

Action

Do you have any pop up temporary structures that you could use to create semi-private spaces? Think about the positioning of the space and how you will encourage the children to explore and develop their own play within it.

A 'dog house' space

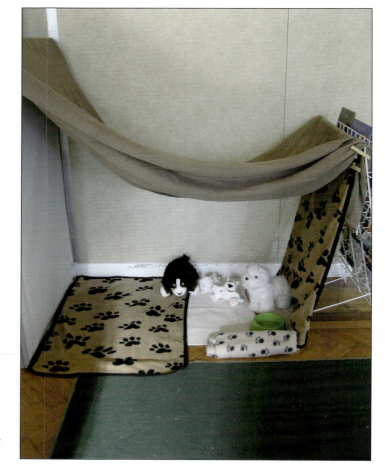

How and why?

We set up a really simple space by attaching a plain drape between two units. The aim of this was to lower the ceiling and add a feeling of cosiness.

The fluffy dog blankets made it feel warm and inviting.

The addition of just a few soft toy dogs and a bowl was enough to trigger some really imaginative play and 'storying'.

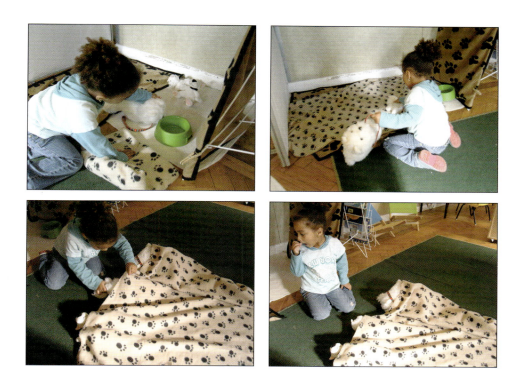

Summer played for a long time in the 'dog house' as she called it. She demonstrated a transporting schema in her play, constantly moving and repositioning the game onto the spare dog blankets in the space. Her play involved lining up the dogs, putting them to bed, taking them for a walk and feeding them. It revolved around the simple space that we had created. She played alone but talked quietly to the dogs. She was completely absorbed in her imaginary world, a place where children's language is "at its most powerful". (Margaret Meek)

Action

What sort of simple spaces could you create to help children to enter their imaginary worlds?

A place to listen

How and why?

We positioned a series of hangings in the trees edging the outside space. We used wind chimes and prisms. The items were there as points of interest, for the children to notice and find. They were carefully selected to provoke thinking and wondering. The chimes made a lovely relaxing noise in the wind while the prisms sparkled in the sun. These resources were stored in a box ready to hang out in different parts of the outside space.

Opportunities for listening are really important. Being outside, can sometimes be the quietest area in a setting. Positioning activities like these should be done with an awareness of what else is going on nearby that could affect the children's ability to notice and engage.

Grace slowly worked her way along the bushes, looking out for the prisms, touching them and choosing her favourite ones. She noticed the chimes as the wind blew. She said little but was very focused on her discoveries.

> **Action**
>
> Do you make the most of your outside space? What could you add to your space to engage children and make them think, ask questions and observe? All of these skills are necessary for good communication skills. Use the quietest places for maximum effect and allow lots of unhurried time for children to notice and explore.

A space in the dark

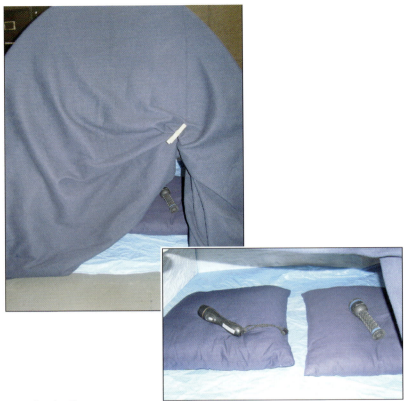

How and why?

This versatile pop up tent has been used inside and outside the setting. It offers an enclosed, robust space that children respond well to. Here we added dark blankets to the structure and provided two torches and cushions.

Louis and Livvy were keen to go inside.

"This is our house," they decided. They quickly turned the torches on.

"I can catch yours."

They played a game of shining their torches at each other's beams.

They closed the doorway and started to whisper.

"Who's knocking at the door" said Louis in a big voice, checking to see if I was still outside. "We need to lock the door. Close the door. I like it closed. It's all dark now."

Changing the lighting in a space can affect the play. It was interesting that a usually quiet child took on a much bolder role in the play when he was private and out of sight.

Action

Try to create a darker space and see if this changes the children's play and language. How can you use light to crate mood and atmosphere in a space?

An enclosed, child height space

How and why?

This setting had a perfect little space under the stairs in which they created a small cosy area. They felt that the hallway was an underused area yet a really quiet spot.

They added footstools to offer alternative seating for the children as well as cushions and a textured rug. They placed some glitter lights in the space, to stimulate investigation.

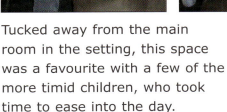

Tucked away from the main room in the setting, this space was a favourite with a few of the more timid children, who took time to ease into the day.

The staff changed the resources in the space to maintain children's interest, but found that it was a great starting place for this group of children.

"They loved the glitter lights and always liked watching them change colour. They came and showed you the lights and it helped the quiet ones start talking to you. We think of this as a discovery place really." Amanda, staff member.

Action

Do you have a special place which quiet children tend to gravitate to? Notice where they spend time. Are there small spaces for children to play and talk? Some children find big groups overwhelming and won't reveal their verbal skills in this context.

A place for a chat

How and why?

We kept this space really simple. We used two dog baskets with soft blankets and cushions and positioned them to encourage interaction. We added a light to define the area and an unusual plant to generate interest. We wanted it to be a place where the children would gather and chat.

The children loved this space. It was certainly a place for social interaction and also rest. Children sought out this space at times during the session when they just wanted to sit and be. So often children are hurried through a series of activities or adult lead routines and yet they need time to take stock and reflect. Having this unhurried time helps them process what is going on around them. This is important so that they feel relaxed. Emotional security in an environment connects significantly with a child's willingness to talk.

Action

Do you have a space like this where children can sit and chat? Think about the positioning of the seating so that the children face each other and can see facial expression and all of the important non verbal clues that other children will give them, to help them understand what is being said.

An instant space

How and why?

This space was created using a clothes horse, a sheet and pegs. It took seconds to set up and yet provided a screened area for children to use. It was positioned next to a window, to make the most of the natural light in the hallway. Natural light is a magical resource that helps us feel more connected, creative and focused.

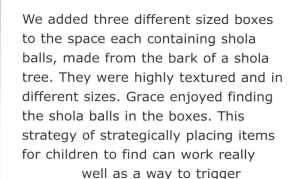

We added three different sized boxes to the space each containing shola balls, made from the bark of a shola tree. They were highly textured and in different sizes. Grace enjoyed finding the shola balls in the boxes. This strategy of strategically placing items for children to find can work really well as a way to trigger conversation and wondering.

She responded particularly well to the corner we created as it reduced the distracting flow of movement in the hallway.

Action

What items could you position for children to find that could trigger conversations? Think carefully about where you place them and how the physical space could then support extended conversations and exploration.

A space for collections

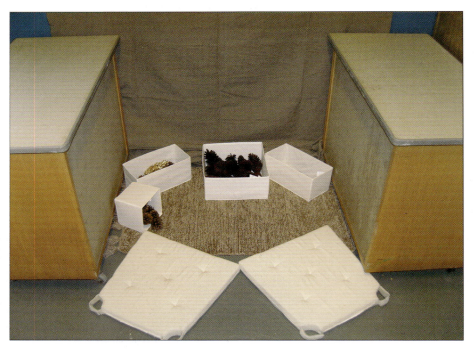

How and why?

Aware of the limited storage in many pack away settings, we used collapsible storage containers to present the cones and conkers that the children had collected on an autumn walk. The two wheeled tray units were positioned to create an alcove area. The rug and cushions encouraged the children to sit and explore.

We added a natural coloured drape to the wall, to add a calmness to the space as the paintwork was bright turquoise.

Dan and Jona spent time investigating.

"They're prickly. They're sharp like scissors. They smell," said Dan.

"These are spiky. They roll," said Jona.

The alcove helped the children to concentrate and not be distracted by the flow of movement in the setting.

Action

How can you position your units and furniture when setting up to create natural alcoves and small spaces where children can congregate away from the distracting flow of movement?

A defined space

How and why?

We made use of the benches in the setting to define and zone the space. The area was deliberately empty of resources to allow the children to add to it what they wanted. We used the light to add a magical feel to the space. We wanted it to be a place where children could gather.

Livvy was fascinated by the light. She stood and watched it for a long time, in awe. She then lay down on the mats and looked up at it. She found the space a really soothing place to reflect.

Action

What systems do you have or could you set up to offer real choice to the children, so that they can manage materials and resources independently?

Action points

Here is a summary of the questions we posed to prompt action. Use them to reflect on the environment that you currently provide for children and then to help you focus on making positive changes.

> Do you have any quiet spaces where children can 'watch' from? Are they comfortable and inviting?

> What sort of resources do you have that children would find as interesting?

> Look at your story area. Does it feel calm and inviting? Would you like to spend time relaxing with a book in there? Do you need to thin out the books and present them more effectively?

> Do you have any pop up temporary structures that you could use to create a semi-private space? Think about the positioning of the space and how you will encourage the children to explore and develop their own play within it.

> What sort of simple spaces could you create to help children to enter their imaginary worlds?

> Do you make the most of your outside space? What could you add to your space to engage children and make them think, ask questions and observe?

> Try to create a darker space and see if this changes the children's play and language. How can you use light to create mood and atmosphere in a space?

> Do you have a special place which quiet children tend to gravitate to? Notice where they spend time. Are there small spaces for children to play and talk? Some children find big groups overwhelming and won't reveal their verbal skills in this context.

> Do you have a space where children can sit and chat? Think about the positioning of seating so that the children face each other and

A Place to Talk *in* Pack-away Settings

can see facial expression and all of the important non verbal clues that other children will give them, to help them understand what is being said.

➢ What items could you position for children to find that could trigger conversations?

➢ How can you position your units and furniture when setting up to create natural alcoves and small spaces where children can congregate away from the distracting flow of movement?

➢ Do you have any spaces that inspire a sense of awe for the children? A space that feels special?

➢ What's your role in supporting children's speaking and listening skills?

Useful resources

The resources that we used to create our 'places to talk' were easy to source and inexpensive. They included:

➢ Net curtains

➢ Blankets in natural, relaxing colours

➢ Textured cushions

➢ Different sized rugs

➢ Interesting objects to stimulate talk, e.g. shola balls, prisms, wind chimes, torches

➢ Drapes to enclose spaces

➢ A pop-up tent

➢ Stacking boxes

➢ Fold flat storage

➢ Clothes horse

➢ Battery operated lighting

➢ Plants

Further references and useful websites

The Communication Friendly Spaces Toolkit: Improving Speaking and Listening Skills in the Early Years Foundation Stage. Jarman, Elizabeth (2007). ISBN: 1-859-90428-9. Can be ordered from Prolog (0870 600 2400)

Cost to the Nation, I CAN, 2006, available from www.ican.org.uk

www.pge.com for information about studies on the way day lighting affects children's learning

Policy for Effective Learning in the Foundation Stage. Jaeckle, S (2002) Bristol City Council Education Department

www.sightlines-initiative.com for information about the Reggio Emilia Children's Network, conferences and resources

www.quietclassrooms.org for guidance on controlling noise in settings and public places

www.colourtest.ue-foundation.org for information on the effects of colours on behaviour

Children, Spaces, Relations: Meta project for an environment for young children, Ceppi, G; Zini, M. (1998) Reggio Children Publications. ISBN: 8-887-96011-9

Other books in this series

A Place to Talk *in* Children's Centres

978 1 906029 27 X

A Place to Talk *in* Extended Schools

978 1 906029 28 8

A Place to Talk *in* Pre-schools

978 1 906029 25 8

all by Elizabeth Jarman

Thanks to all of the settings and practitioners who informed and inspired this publication, especially:

Abacus Play Group, Nottinghamshire

St.John's Play Group, Bournemouth